Goodbye Clutter, Hello Freedom

How to create space for Danish Hygge
and Lifestyle by cleaning up,
organizing, and decorating with care

Lena Bentsen

*Danish Life Designer, life skilled expert in
Danish Lifestyle and Hygge*

ISBN-13: 978-1542764100
ISBN-10: 1542764106

Printed in the United States of America

Why did I write this book?

I am a Danish Life Designer living in Denmark and because of this, Danish Hygge and lifestyle are deeply anchored in my DNA.

I wrote this book because I want to help you experience the amazing feeling of freedom that comes from living in a home that reflects the best part of you. I want to help you create a home that is easy to clean up and built on the foundation of Danish Hygge.

Why should you read this book?

You should read this book if you want a shortcut to a home that supports your well-being and is almost free of clutter. If you are curious about the magic of Hygge and decluttering the Danish way or tired of feeling inadequate because of to-do lists left unwritten, this book is for you. If you cannot stand feeling homeless in your own home, I can help you.

This book will help you with…

In this book, you will learn techniques to clean up the Danish way. It will help you to know what to get rid of and what to save. You will learn tools and techniques to help you focus on why and how to sort through your stuff and how to maintain daily order in an easy way.

This is the ultimate guidebook to help you create a personal home that suits you with your best treasures - a home ready to help you create the mood of Danish Hygge, and a life with more freedom. Learning to clean up the Danish way will certainly help you to think in a new way, one that definitely works.

What some readers have to say

"Bentsen focuses less on the mechanics than on changing your perspective: realizing that to care for yourself, you must care for your space. This [book] has changed my thinking – and thus my actions and my space – more in a week than all the other "tidying up" books in my universe combined." – Cynthia

"Since reading this book, our house is lovely now, always clean and enjoyable to live in, and we even let friends drop in unannounced without worrying about how the house looks anymore. It's literally changed our lives." – Chris

"Written from the perspective of a Danish native, this book carries with it a certain heart and soul that you don't normally find in a how-to. Very easy to understand and apply." – Morgyn

"I like the way that the author explains everything – it makes so much sense and there is a lot of information here that I haven't found anywhere else. Valuable and inspiring read!" – Louise

"I have read many decluttering books, but this one spoke to me in a different way. Lena's approach to tidying and organising was kind and caring, rather than judgemental. It was simple and logical and to the point and it feels so do-able." – Amazon Customer

"I have read many books about declutter, so far only Lena's book gave me the reasons and motivation to start. This is a life changing book." – Che-Hsiung Liuon

About The Author

Lena Bentsen, born in 1954, is known as "The Grand Old Lady" in the Danish decluttering business. In 2005, she started the organizational wave in Denmark. As a trained Feng Shui interior designer, she also knows, feels, and sees the details of a space that can provide or disrupt the feeling of wellbeing.

As a native Dane, Danish Hygge flows in her veins and is a part of her DNA. Over her lifetime, Lena Bentsen has become intimately familiar with every Danish tradition. As a Danish Life Designer, she paints the picture of the deepest essence of Danish Hygge and the typical Danish way of life.

Lena Bentsen is a famous author in Denmark, having written five books about these topics. She and her work are often exposed in the media.

Table of Contents

A Foreword about Danish Hygge and Clutter

Maybe you have heard that Danish people are among the happiest people in the world. It is true, but we are not born that way. It is in our culture, and it can be learned.

Summer in Denmark is very short: about 10 weeks. And often, it is not even that long. Here, autumn, winter, and spring dominate the calendar. And even worse, because rain, wind, very short days, and long nights abound, we have to do something to survive. We have to Hygge.

Hygge is a strange concept to describe, but really, it is mostly about focusing on positive details in life. Details that put you in a good mood. The Danes care about details.

We create the Hygge mood, which helps us survive through periods of bad weather. Even when the weather turns good for a short period, we still continue to Hygge. All year around.

Social gatherings with friends almost always take place at home and that's why we, as a nation, are exceedingly passionate about our homes.

All living spaces are visual pictures that can tell you a lot about the people who live there. If the house is overrun with clutter, it tells you that whoever lives there probably do not care much about the details in life. But, maybe they do care, and just do not know how to show it in their home. Perhaps, they simply did not learn how or why to show that they care about details. In this book, we will start with the most obvious way to show that you do care: your house.

Welcome

This is the e-book that will finally help you overcome the past challenges that you have had with clutter or disorder. There is hope.

Many people have already been taught to say "goodbye" to their clutter and "hello" to a life filled with freedom, Danish Hygge, and a better overall outlook. So, why should there not be hope for you as well?

Remember, it is all about helping you create a home that paints a good picture of who you are or want to be. The amount of order that you need will be unique. Only you can know what kind of home will bring you that great feeling of freedom.

Bringing order to your home will help motivate you to get the cleanup started. If you have no idea what your proverbial carrot is, there is absolutely no reason to begin the huge hassle of cleaning up. You must have a goal worth aiming for. Without one, you might as well just do nothing.

"Order means freedom"

It is no coincidence that the title of this book is *Goodbye Clutter, Hello Freedom*. Your freedom is at stake. When you start cleaning up your life, you will experience a larger and larger sense of freedom. I will help you through with humor and a hand to hold.

I hope that through order, you have the best of luck in finding all of the good things in your life that are hiding.

You Are Not Alone

Do you dream of a life filled with freedom? A life that allows you to relax and just enjoy yourself with your mind at ease? A life where you can spread out your arms and breathe freely and deeply, knowing you have lots of extra energy? Do you dream of a life of order with space for Hygge?

To give you complete confidence that you are in the right place with the right book, here are a few questions from me:

- *Are you running away from your clutter?*
- *Are you embarrassed when receiving unexpected guests?*
- *Do you spend time feeling guilty about not cleaning up?*
- *Do you not feel 'at home'?*

Would you like to learn a more fun and entertaining way to organize your home? If you are ready to say goodbye to your clutter and hello to the dream of freedom, to Danish Hygge and simple order, then continue reading.

We will go through techniques to help you know how and what to clear out as well as, how and what to save. For saving techniques, you will get advice on how and where to store things.

First and foremost, I write to all of my global sisters because we normally take care of the domestic side of life. But, dear men, I would be thrilled if you would read along. I am sure that you would also benefit greatly from the content of this book. So, fellow sisters/brothers, you are on your way.

I am Quite Normal

Let it be said right away: I am surely just as lazy as you. Are you disappointed or relieved?

Most probably, I have as many things to do in my daily life as you: a job, children, shopping, cleaning, and cooking. On top of all that, in the name of equality, we women often also: keep the garden, wash the car and do other odd jobs such as changing light bulbs or gaskets inside and outside.

We have enough to do. Do not forget that we also need time for exercising, postgraduate courses, and socializing, all the while being an attractive wife or girlfriend.

Oh yes, there is never a risk that a housewife might be out of work. Hooray for that! I have quite a normal life, just like you, with all of the necessary tasks. However, I would also like to have time for the things that really make me feel happy and alive. I want to Hygge.

Because, like you, I am trying to balance necessary daily work and the fun that life has to offer, I have found that it is necessary to focus on prioritizing the things around me. I have had to closely examine which items really mean something positive to me. I have also had to learn how to get rid of the things that do not mean anything to me or maybe even have a negative effect on me.

Please do not think that this means that I am missing anything from my life. Definitely not. That is exactly what this book is about: how to make room for more of the best in life by cleaning up, organizing, and eventually creating Danish Hygge.

Room for Fun

As previously mentioned, this book is a guide for anyone who would like to have more fun in life without giving up on anything important. I bet that you will experience a greater richness as you get rid of everything that has no value to you and put the rest into a truly usable system.

By learning some new techniques for thoroughly cleaning up and prioritizing your time so that you can keep yourself organized every day, you will find that you have much more time for fun and Hygge. Believe me. You will have no more anxiety about your home, you will be able to spontaneously invite friends over without a second thought, and you will dare to welcome unexpected guests without hesitation.

You will be able to take an unplanned day off with a good conscience. You will know how to spontaneously buy the right things in order to beautify yourself, your home, and your life.

In short, you are going to be the master of your own life. Once you know what you appreciate, where your stuff is, and can understand the difference between what is good and what is bad for you to own, you will be free to enjoy the life that you truly deserve.

"You will find that you have plenty of time left to be YOU"

During the course of this book, you may wonder how on earth I know what you have in your drawers and closets, how you think and act, what things you are hiding, and why you are not moving on.

I am neither psychic nor possess other supernatural abilities, but I am very familiar with this situation. I know about it because of my own life and because of all the other people whom I have helped out of the clutter and into order and freedom. Trust me.

I am absolutely convinced that you are not any different from the rest. On the contrary, I can assure you that you are quite normal. Therefore, I also know that with help, you can move on to a life with more order and a better overall outlook.

"Messy people are simply people who do not know how to maintain order"

You have to learn how to clean up

When I was a child, my mum ordered me to clean up; but how on earth could I know how to do it if I had never learned? Big problem. It was not until I reached a grown up age that I was able to crack the code on clutter and find my way to order.

In this the book, you will learn how to clean up and maintain order. You will find all of the help that you need to face your clutter and free yourself from the mess. You can skip the hassle of learning on your own and stumbling through unfamiliar territory, help has arrived.

Good luck clearing the way towards a new and more enjoyable life.

Who Lives Here?

Our home is a snitch and tells everything about who we are as individuals and how we manage our lives. Just stop and take a look around. If you came into your own home for the first time, what would you think?

Take a picture of your home

A photograph is honest and reveals all. It can be an eye opener to take some pictures of your home. Pay attention to what you notice most in the pictures. What catches your eye? Our eyes will always focus on imperfection, on what breaks the flow of the image.

Now ask yourself: *Is this my home?* If you are not completely satisfied with the answer, there is only one thing to do. Get started cleaning up. The joy of order is great, actually bigger than you think. This will work for you too, but it requires a decision and a good dose of discipline.

"Order does not develop by itself like clutter does"

You need to create and incorporate regular routines that eliminate clutter before it begins to pile up. You brush your teeth every day because, at some point, you realized that it pays to keep your teeth clean. In the same way, you must clean up every day because it pays off.

If you constantly make sure that you do not leave clutter in your wake, fortunately, not much will pile up and it will actually not be that hard to clean. I will get back to how you can go about daily cleaning up. But for now, we need to concentrate on developing a home that really represents you. First, we have to take an eye-opening journey in order to understand the spirit of order and clutter.

What Is an Orderly Home?

I am not advocating that our homes should be so tidy that it is no longer obvious who lives there. Of course, a home should clearly declare who it was that created it. Otherwise, instead of being a home, it would just be a place. A home must reflect the best aspects of who lives there; otherwise, you and your home are not really connected.

"There is a big difference between living in clutter and living with personality"

Our home is the place where we gather energy. It is where we relax, enjoy ourselves, and spend most of our time. It should, therefore, bring us the best of the best. Home should be our breathing space, where we just enjoy being. This is why you need to put an end to your clutter. Clutter brings you nothing of value; on the contrary, it only makes things worse.

Try to imagine that you could listen to your clutter. Imagine that is sounds like a discordant orchestra, with each musician playing his own distorted sound, or it might sound like a radio that is only able to receive 35 radio stations at the same time. Help. You would probably hurry up and leave. This is what your clutter does to you. You cannot hear it, but you can feel it.

You might be able to ignore this jarring feeling, but it is still there, lurking in your subconscious. It makes you want to escape your home just to get away from your clutter. But, do not try to escape. Do not give your mess the power to determine your whereabouts.

You need to make your home into a place where you enjoy being. Just as it is important to love your daily life, you should be able to love living it in your home.

Our Surroundings Affect Us

Whether we want to admit it or not, we are affected by our surroundings. The old saying, "the clothes make the man" could just as well say, "surroundings make the man." Our behavior changes according to our surroundings and circumstances. In a museum, we walk nicely and quietly. On a picnic it is okay to fool around and get dirty.

When it is already messy, we give up in advance on putting things in place and might end up simply putting them in whatever pile is nearest. In orderly surroundings, we tend to behave in a more orderly fashion.

We are the direct result of our environment. If our home looks like something that does not matter, we behave in the same way. Crumbs might get thrown on the floor, elbows will be well planted on the table while eating, and it will not matter if we spill. We become indifferent.

Danish Hygge is about caring, and when we do not care for our surroundings, clutter begins to spread its way into our lives, and Hygge is no longer a possibility.

The 12 Truths About Clutter

It is not always pleasant to listen to the truth, but not spoken out loud, you will never have to treat it. I dare you to focus on it.

TRUTH NO. 1

Clutter sneaks up on you

Clutter sneaks up on you quietly, without a sound. Suddenly, it is there and has taken over your life. Many people claim they are comfortable with their clutter, but I doubt that it is true. I do not believe that they are comfortable with the clutter, as much as they are comfortable with keeping the many things that surround them.

"Clutter is made of things that are not getting any attention"

Children become hard to handle when they do not get enough attention. The same thing happens with clutter. Though we cannot hear it, we can feel it. It makes life hard on us by draining our energy, mood, and our will to live in general. Your mess has probably also sneaked up on you. Quietly, without a sound, it has grown from disorder to clutter, bringing chaos into your life.

I wonder if you have started to organize many times. Maybe you have cleaned up here and there, but stalled while you desperately wondered what to do with this thing or that. You might have bought storage boxes in various sizes and materials. Even though you have probably thrown out some bags, the effect of the cleanup has been minor.

TRUTH NO. 2

Two types of clutter

There are two kinds of clutter: Active clutter and passive clutter.

You are probably reading this book because you have quite a lot of passive clutter and you would like to do away with it. In the beginning, it was just a collection of different things that you were using. This is active clutter. They became passive clutter the very moment that you no longer needed them and forgot to put them away. That is how a pile of items actually turns into clutter.

It is active clutter when the youngest in the family turns his LEGO-box upside down. However, the creative process does not last. His focus shifts and after a few hours or days other things will occupy him. At that moment the active clutter turns into passive clutter and the cleanup can start.

When you cook you will make active clutter. But, if you do not clean up 100 % when the meal is finished, you will have created passive clutter.

TRUTH NO. 3

Clutter is immobile

Things cannot move themselves. When you no longer need to have your things out, you need to return them to their places. Whether or not they want to, they cannot move themselves. If the mess does not get any help, it becomes clutter.

TRUTH NO. 4

Clutter is lack of caring

Caring for our things is as simple as remembering to put them away when we no longer need them. When we react to our surroundings with care, we also care for ourselves. We are a reflection of our surroundings and if we do not care for them, it has a negative effect on us.

"Our surroundings are a part of us"

The good news is that we can deliberately change this situation. When we start to clean and organize our homes, something bigger begins to happen. We influence our surroundings. In the same way that failing to maintain our homes affects us in a negative way, when we begin to care about our surroundings, it affects us in a positive way.

TRUTH NO. 5

Clutter drains your energy

Clutter reinforces itself. It drains you of energy so that you do not bother to clean up.

"The chicken or the egg: What comes first, clutter or the lack of energy?"

Is it the clutter draining you of energy, or do you produce clutter because you lack energy?

We all experience times in life when we do not have the energy to do much more than just care for ourselves. During these times just getting up and making a bit of food is a challenge. Clutter definitely does not make a situation like this better. Quite the contrary.

TRUTH NO. 6

Clutter smells

Are you aware that mess smells? When things are not being used, they do not get fresh air and start to smell stale.

There is a reason that we need fresh air. You have probably had the urge to get out and just breathe some good air. A brisk walk can do wonders. Fresh air is necessary for us in many ways.

Everything that we own also needs fresh air to stay alive. Think about when the seasons change and it is time to get out your jackets, the ones that have hung in the closet for months. Although they are clean, they do not smell good anymore. They need fresh air, almost as if they have gotten bad breath.

Often, I experience the same smell when I first enter a home in order to help create better organization. When things have been hidden for a long time and they have not been exposed to fresh air, they start to smell stale. When you clean up, it is therefore a good idea to air your things out. Remember to go outside yourself and get some fresh air. Otherwise, you will inhale the 'bad breath' of your things.

From my own world - "When I was a child on summer holiday in the countryside at my grandparents place, and the weather one day showed its sunny side, clotheslines were hung throughout the yard. It was time to air. Duvets, pillows, and other bedding were brought out. The big black coats from the closets and several rugs were brought out to hang, to be 'aired', as my grandmother said."

TRUTH NO. 7

Clutter endangers health

Of course, you can stumble or trip over clutter and break your leg. However, when you are surrounded by it, you will also lose sight of the bigger picture. When that picture is gone, we seem to become stressed easier. When we are stressed, a particular hormone is released in the body that weakens our immune system over time.

Dust, dirt, debris, and other filthy things thrive in and around clutter because disorganization can prevent you from cleaning. When you find yourself surrounded like this, you may also find that it is more difficult to muster the motivation to clean up. All in all, this is an environment in which infectious diseases can develop.

TRUTH NO. 8

Clutter makes you feel guilty

Be honest. You probably got this book because you know that you ought to clean up.

Am I correct in guessing that you wanted to start this a long time ago, but have never gotten to the bottom of it? Maybe you have never really even started? There is nothing like a bad conscience draining us of energy.

We know that we should start cleaning up, but we keep on postponing it. As a result, we get frustrated and disappointed for betraying ourselves, and all the while we are still not able to start the project that could turn all of the negative feelings around. The energy is pouring out of us and with it, the joy of life.

TRUTH NO. 9

Clutter makes you embarrassed

While the struggles attached to clutter drain your energy down to zero, there is also an embarrassment attached to the problem. You become ashamed of yourself and cannot look yourself in the eyes. And because you are so ashamed of how bad things have really become, it becomes unthinkable to let others see your struggle. This makes it difficult to invite guests over because you worry about what they will think! In a downward spiral like this, depression is lurking right around the corner.

> *Benn, 57, Copenhagen - "I am so ashamed of my mess that neither my friends nor children have visited me for several years. A few years ago, I was seriously ill with pneumonia and called the doctor. He wanted to come and examine me, but I rejected him and did not allow him into my mess. Because I was too embarrassed to let the doctor in, it nearly cost me my life."*

TRUTH NO. 10

Clutter costs time and money

When we do not have an overall understanding of where our belongings are, we do not stand a chance of knowing what is in the cupboards. Is there enough pasta? How about canned tomatoes or flour? Or, why not buy an extra blouse?

When we do not know where things are in our homes, we are obviously not aware of what we own. We keep adding new possessions instead of finding the ones that we already have.

Lacking an overview or inventory of items leads to random purchases here and there. When we go to the store, we try to use the best of our knowledge. We randomly buy bits and pieces because we think that they will transform our living room into a dream.

The truth is that it will only contribute to the clutter because too many things are already adding to the confusion. Only when things are organized and you can really know what you need, is it time to accentuate the mood with nicer items.

TRUTH NO. 11

Clutter strains relationships

If you and your partner cannot find something else to argue about, you can always argue about who makes the most mess and who has not cleaned up. While you are at it, why not also criticize the children, the dog, or the mother-in-law? Clutter can cause fuses to be short and can add to preexisting relationship issues.

> *Lone, 36, Jutland, "We had rebuilt and now had a lovely house with room for our two wonderful children and ourselves - and all our mess. The mess was draining us. My husband could not bear to leave the car and walk inside when coming home from work and even I got socially involved outside the home to have an excuse to not be at home. We did not realize how much the mess affected our relationship - until we cleaned up."*

TRUTH NO. 12

Clutter requires attention

Are you aware that you are storing information about everything in your home? Everything the eye can see. We will do a little experiment: If you have a bookshelf, select a book in your head. It does not matter which, simply select one.

Now, answer the following questions:

- *Is it big or small? Is it new or old?*
- *Is it a hard or soft cover?*
- *Where or when did you get it?*
- *Do you remember anything from the book?*
- *Does it have a smell? Is it heavy or light?*

Honestly, are you not surprised at how much you know about a random book? Here comes the scary part: you know something about everything around you. Of course, it is not all as clear as the book you just thought about, but if we open up to it, we know at least something about everything that we own.

Now, here comes the *really* bad part: If you are surrounded by clutter, your memory is constantly working overtime. For example, you have to remember that the papers from the landlord are in that pile, the bill that you need to check from the utility company is in that pile, the thing for repairing is in that pile over there, and so on. You even know something about all of the things that you have put away.

It is no wonder that you are feeling tired and exhausted and have no energy to begin cleaning up.

The Purpose of Order

I assume that all of this information about clutter has resonated with you on some personal level. I imagine that you have been able to recognize some of your own problems in the things that have been discussed. Maybe you were not fully aware that it was actually the disorganization making it easy for you to fight with your partner, or that it was your clutter repeatedly causing the colds and flu. We are going to approach this from a different perspective and look at the wonderful things that order has to offer you.

To clean up is to look yourself in the eyes

It might be a bit bold to claim that your order or lack thereof is a reflection of your life in a ratio of 1:1, but I am going to risk it. Your job, clothes, social circle, home, children, and finances – all of these create an image of who you are. The good news is that the image is changeable.

Once you start confronting your stuff, it is the same as confronting your life. You start taking responsibility for your own life. Once you dare to face yourself, you can act upon it.

This process can have many aspects, but a common feature is that whatever it is that is blocking the path to your dream is a separate issue that you have not yet confronted.

By cleaning up, you make a carefree environment. There are no hidden issues giving you a bad conscience just because you choose to go feed ducks with the kids instead of cleaning up. You have already cleaned up. You are free to do what you want.

You do not have to waste time looking for lost items. You know where your things are. Your time can be spent doing something nice.

Once you know how your financial situation is, you do not have to be afraid of getting letters from the bank or worse. You are free. You are sitting in the driver's seat.

"Freedom means taking control of your time"

Once you have order and a real grasp on your life and belongings, you can take charge of your own life and save a lot of money on things like therapists, comfort shopping, and penalty fees. You can save yourself from spending hours on pointless frustrations. With the money and time that you have saved, you can simply focus on having a wonderful life. You could afford to go on vacation. You can do whatever you want.

You will have time to read and play with the kids, to be a good partner, and to embrace your life. You will have time to be free. You will have time to Hygge.

To clean up is to give yourself a home

One of the most important benefits of cleaning up is that it can transform your home into the welcoming, relaxing place that you have always wanted. Your home is a representative of YOU and should be a reflection of you. It should be a place where you can relax and gather energy. It should be able to embrace and accommodate you. You can enjoy Hygge.

It is not for me to decide or to advise you on what you should save or get rid of. Only you know what emotions are connected to your things and only you can decide what to do with them. You will learn that later.

Function or feeling

I sincerely encourage you to start dividing things on your own. Decide which items YOU believe belong in your home. A beautiful stone that was picked up on a beach could fill your heart with so much joy that keeping it is the only option. Only you know! If it is so important, it MUST have a place in your home.

You know the story behind each of your belongings. Only you know if they give you a good feeling inside or not. The important thing is finding the ones that do just that.

Your home is your center of energy, where you experience freedom and joy. In order to find freedom and joy in your home, you should focus on surrounding yourself only with things that add something positive.

You have to care about your stuff. You have to really, truly care because everything that you own was invited by you into your life to help you in some way. They might look smart, give you a good feeling, help you cook, or simply help you live your life. No matter what you look at, it should give you a sense of caring.

"Ask yourself: Does the function or feeling support me in a positive way?"

You should, therefore, get rid of everything related to bad memories or simply associated with the slightest indifference. Once you confront yourself with each of your things, you will know that they are there to please you; otherwise, they are not good for you.

The 3 Categories of "Clear Out"

If you have decided to get even with your clutter, you have also decided to get rid of a whole lot of things. Otherwise, you simply will not get any closer to your goal.

As you read on, you will find that I frequently say, "OUT", and it might sound a little harsh to you. When I make a declaration like that, I mean that whatever thing you are considering must be expelled from your life and your home. If a particular item is still usable, there are always alternatives to throwing it in the trash. I do not want to encourage wastefulness, only thoughtfulness.

At the same time, I would like to point out that a lot of what we save in our homes is unfortunately nothing but garbage. For many things, it would be impossible to find someone who would want to take them off your hands. The only word for something like that is: "OUT"!

Things to remove from your life can roughly be divided into 3 categories:

- *Recyclable things*
- *Valuable things to be sold*
- *Waste*

1. Recyclable things

There are many charities that happily accept clothes and other things that are nice, clean, and functional. Find the organizations in your area that accept these kinds of donations. There are even groups and second-hand dealers who will pick up bigger items, so you do not have to bother with moving them.

You do not necessarily need to donate to typical charities like the Red Cross. A day care or kindergarten near your home would probably be very excited by a donation of some of your children's best, discarded toys, or whatever else they might need. Just make sure that they are good, clean, functional items.

The most important thing to remember when you decide to recycle or donate items is to act quickly. Gather everything in a bag or suitable container and pass it on as soon as possible. Otherwise, it could pile up and become more clutter.

If you are giving your things away to others, it could require solving some logistical problems.

Since you are taking the initiative, it might be reasonable for you to be in charge of the transportation. If so, you should take action immediately, the sooner the better. You cannot leave clutter piling up when you are about to move into a new, orderly life.

One thing to remember: Only give things away to willing recipients. Do not pass on your clutter to people who are only accepting it to be polite.

"Passing on clutter is not allowed!"

Also, remember not to take on clutter from others. Do not accept something because you think that it might be nice or usable in the future. It will not.

2. Valuable things to be sold

For things of value, it might be a good idea to first determine whether or not it would be worth the effort of selling.

Keep in mind that the process of selling might be a bit slow. Consider whether price is worth the hassle of storing the items, maybe for months, before they are sold. This has the potential to create new clutter. On top of that, if they need repair before being sold, you should really consider the situation carefully to make sure that you are not wasting your time and effort.

You must be honest with yourself and ask the question, "Will I have this finished within a couple of days?" If you cannot confidently answer with a yes, you should let others take over to ensure that you move forward in the process. For example, send that beautiful, old chair to an expert for re-upholstering so that it can be sold. Just make sure that the value of the refurbished chair will make it worth your while.

Remember, by giving to charity you are donating. It might be better to give something away than to try to sell it.

3. Waste

Do not be surprised to find that a lot of your clutter is normal waste: newspapers, magazines, envelopes, things that are broken or useless, clothes, boots, handbags etc.

Your clutter, in many cases, developed because you have put things in the wrong places. Instead of throwing them in the dumpster, you happened to put them in the basement or attic, hoping that they would be of value again one day.

This rarely happens, so just start sorting.

> *Poul, Sealand, "Being a child during the Second World War, I know only too well that you do not throw anything out that might be useful. In 1972, we moved from our two-bedroom apartment into a new, lovely detached house. Although we bought new furniture, we brought many of the old pieces, putting them directly in the attic. There was more than enough space. With difficulty, we even put an old freezer up in the attic. Today, I wonder how we got it up there, not to mention, what I thought we would use it for. We had already bought a new one."*

The Big Decision

Figuring out what to do with the things that you choose to part with is only one obstacle. Another, much bigger problem is reaching the point when you choose to say goodbye at all. All of the things in your home are things that you bought for a reason.

"Ask the object, How positive an impact do you have on me?"

Only save items that will truly have a positive impact on you and your future. If you would like a home that fills you with joy and gives you energy, focus on what every surrounding thing contributes.

In the future, when you are in doubt about whether or not to buy something for your home, try to chat a bit with the object about the positive effect that it could have on your life.

Make the decision and forgive yourself

First, you must make your intentions clear to yourself and really consider the process that you are about to start. Look around and admit what the root cause of the clutter is. Forgive yourself for letting it go this far and focus on moving forward.

Visualize your home as it will be once you are done. Imagine how it will feel once it is cleaned up.

Decide how you are going to reward yourself through the process. You will probably not be done in one day, so set goals and decide how to celebrate. Maybe you would like a holiday, a new pair of shoes, or fresh flowers to go on the windowsill.

NOW is the right time

Have you already made the big decision to get started? If not, do it now. What is the worst that could happen if you put it off? What is the best thing that could happen if you dive in?

Is there any reason not to? I can only think of a few. You can decide for yourself how important they are.

- *Laziness: when you just do not bother cleaning up.*
- *Intimidation: if you do not dare to confront it and would rather leave it.*

However, I do not believe that you are here because you are lazy or afraid of confrontation. You are here because you are ready to say goodbye to your clutter and create a life full of freedom and Hygge.

You might as well face it; nobody else will take care of this for you. Your clutter remains your responsibility and it is time to do something about it. NOW. Perhaps you have neglected it for years, all the while wondering how to fix it and wanting to find answers.

But, the perfect day when that right amount of energy and motivation came together, the weather was decent, and the stars were aligned never happened. Until now.

Do you know why? A more 'perfect moment' will never come and it will never get better than NOW.

"The right moment to get started is NOW!"

NOW is always the right time. Whether it is today, tomorrow, or in two weeks, because a week with two Thursdays will never come. So, the only thing you need to do is start cleaning up. You only waste time by waiting. This is your own time, your own life.

I cannot make the decision for you. Only you know if you have had enough of your clutter. Remember, you got this book because you wanted to change something in your life. I promise that I will be with you the whole way, helping you as much as you want.

Are you ready to make the big decision? You must answer right now. Yes, or no. Did I hear a huge YES?

How to Get Sta

When

It can be difficult to really envision how
this can be. It will require some preparation. First and
foremost, it is important to start off nice and easy. Do not
be discouraged by what you see right now. I promise that
you will come to feel the euphoria of freedom. All it takes
is slightly different behavior.

It is perfectly acceptable to set big goals for yourself, like
clearing an entire room, and then celebrate your progress
with a reward. But, whatever goal you set must be
separated into bite-sized pieces, otherwise you might run
out of steam. The task should be approachable.

One of the first things we are going to address is focusing
on one thing at a time. I really do mean one thing at a
time; I am talking about each actual detail and each
physical item. It would be too overwhelming to think of a
whole room at once. You must focus on one detail, such
as the pen in your hand right now. You can only touch one
thing at a time. Once you allow yourself to do one small
thing, it is much easier to continue to the next.

If you want to experience freedom, you need to let
yourself feel like you have accomplished something, like
you are progressing towards your goal. For this to be
possible, you must promise yourself to check off a small
job every day. Something small is not so scary.

you continue with many little things, the results suddenly seem much bigger. The big cleanup consists of lots and lots of tiny pieces.

Everything in its own place

Everything in the universe has its own place. Molecules have their place. The stars have their place in the sky. Anything else would be a mess...

"One of the secrets behind order is the idea of permanent places"

Each of your things has their proper place as well. It is when things are not put in place that clutter develops. It is that simple. It may sound a bit rigid, but actually it is much easier to clean up once you realize that everything has and should have its own permanent place.

All of your things live somewhere and you have to know their place of residence in order to follow them home. This is the only way to find them. They cannot walk by themselves; you have to help them!

Otherwise, they end up as clutter – just stray things moving from one place to another. It can drain you of your energy even with the best of intentions! Clutter is a collection of homeless items, crying out for a place to stay. They are waiting to be taken home and put into place.

"Ask your thing: Where do you live?"

Talking with your belongings might sound like a simple, childish joke. But trust me, you will be surprised to learn where many of them live. It works. Look around right now and find three homeless things just by asking them.

Look for items that you have moved around many times or that have been placed on windowsills or shelves because you did not know where else to put them.

Everything that remains living with you must have a place. Otherwise, it is OUT.

Storage

If all things must have a permanent place, then there must be an actual space to put them. A good intention is useless if you have no real place to keep something.

> *Karina and Mark, South Jutland - Karina and Mark had bought an old villa together. Mark was a carpenter, so the delightful renovation could easily begin. Two years later they had a lovely house with nice, new windows. The only things missing were some walls, and numerous doors, not to mention cupboards, including in the kitchen, which only had a table. And it stayed this way for a long time. Karina and Mark had NO places to put their things. Even their marriage suffered from the lack of cupboards.*

The good news is that you will need less and less storage space as you clean up. Nevertheless, you will require a certain, inescapable minimum of storage solutions.

There must be room for all of your clothes including warm sweaters and winter jackets. The same goes for the entire family, not just you. There must be solutions for everything, from boxes for the children's toys to folders where bills and receipts can be filed. Even the gym bag needs a permanent place. There is no escaping that this all requires a great deal of planning.

All this means that you simply need a certain number of cupboards, shelves, boxes, folders, and drawers. As you clean up, you will find out exactly what your needs are.

Short-term parking: the temporary solution

"Wave-clutter" is the wave of homeless things that is pushed in front of you as you start cleaning up. These are items that need to be moved from one room to another and cannot be put in their places immediately. You cannot do it all at once and it might be that these things are not ready to have a place. Yet.

Wave-clutter happens when your belongings have been displaced temporarily, pending further processing. The question is: what are you supposed to do with them? If you put anything down randomly, it will only increase the amount of clutter in that place.

"Transit boxes for short-term parking are the solution"

If you do not already have some in your household, I recommend that you buy a stack of A3-sized folding plastic boxes in a uniform color. They are so practical because they can be stacked or folded when not in use and they serve many purposes.

When you need to park an item (remember: only short-term parking is allowed) put it in one of the folding boxes, which we will refer to as a transit box. The transit boxes must be identical as you will immediately know that it is only a transit box and not a new storage unit.

You will quickly learn which rooms need transit boxes. When something is moved from one room to another, you should immediately know where to put it. Therefore, the box should be easily recognizable and have a temporarily permanent place.

At the first possible opportunity whatever has been put in the box needs to be moved to its own place. The box must be emptied regularly so that it does not just turn into clutter. Avoid this.

Summary

Now you know:

- *That the perfect time to clean up is always right now.*
- *That you only need to focus on one thing at a time.*
- *That the task must be approachable.*
- *That everything needs a place to stay.*
- *That you should ask your things where they live and bring them home.*
- *That only short-term parking is allowed.*

Next, we will discuss all of the difficult things. These are items that, though you cannot explain why, you are having a hard time giving up. These are blocks, keeping you from getting through the cleanup.

We will deal with them one by one in the next chapter. You will find that this list is a great tool and you have to promise me that whenever you become stuck in your process, you will return to it. You will probably be able to personally identify with a lot of things from the list. Believe me, you will be challenged. There is a reason why you did not say goodbye to your clutter a long time ago, despite the fact that you should have.

Promise me that you will always remember that <u>you</u> are in charge of your things, not vice versa.

The Blocks

There will be quite a large number of things for you to make decisions about in the near future. Though, it will be easy to decide what to do with some items, you will encounter a lot of blocks.

Blocks are things that are difficult for you to get rid of, even if they are no longer being used and never will be again. Once you have made the decision to start cleaning up, you also have to make the decision to get rid of a lot of your belongings. It is not always easy.

You will encounter a number of blocks on your way. You will feel divided about them; you will feel good about some and bad about others. Blocks can bring back memories from your past and they can challenge you about the future.

You will probably experience tears, which you might expect from saying goodbye to your things. In reality, it is likely that it will be because of the big relief associated with clearing them out. It will be a tremendous relief to let go of stuff that has held you down, maybe over a lifetime.

"Blocks can evoke strong, personal feelings"

Many of the blocks involve feelings. You can call it regard for others, your or your family's expectations, or whatever you want. But, the bottom line is that these are things that, for one reason or another, are no longer in harmony with you.

Your feelings and conscience prevent you from moving forward. You will get help with this right now. The cleaning that you are about to do will be a very intimate elimination of pent up emotion. You have to get rid of many things and while you will keep fewer items, they will all be important.

In the following section, we are only going to look at belongings that must leave your home. Remember, I do not decide what to get rid of and what to save. Only you are in charge of this project. You can be sure of this because, though I will challenge you thoroughly, I will show you that these blocks do not rule your life.

"As much as is useful, as little as is necessary"

I will address many things that tend to be tough when deciding what should stay and what needs to go. This saying might be useful along the way:

Things exceeding the expiry date

Everything has an expiry date. I really mean EVERYTHING.

We have a lifelong partnership with some things and the expiry date for those will be the same as our own, but the vast majority of your clutter has probably exceeded its limit. If you do not use them, there is nothing in it for you anymore. The end. You have used up the thing.

"Everything has an expiry date"

When something is no longer being used or loved, for whatever reason, you are no longer beneficial to one another. It is of no use to you and you are of no use to it. You do not have a mutual path anymore and it is time to separate.

If you do not get rid of whatever it is, it will start to drain you of energy. You will get annoyed with it and feel guilty for not having made the decision to throw it out. The thing owns you now, instead of vice versa. It has become a parasite.

"Change focus from 'Can I use...' to 'Can I do without...'"

If you want to succeed in overcoming your clutter, you need to change focus from the concept of 'using' to 'doing without'. You have surely kept this thing only because you thought that you would use it again sometime. This kind of thinking will do you no good if you want to have an orderly home.

It is about focusing on the possibility of doing without this thing. The simple question, 'Can I do without?' will make you realize how much junk you have lying around. You will find that you do not use these items anymore and can easily do without them.

Here comes the first challenge: Get rid of it. Items that you have stopped using do not serve any purpose in your life. You have used up the whole thing. It is of no use anymore. It is done.

Because the thing cannot disappear by itself, you must help it to get out of your life. NOW.

"Things that are too good to throw out"

I can almost hear you say how sure you are that you will miss this thing in two weeks. You are absolutely right.

In the next two weeks, maybe in a month, you will probably think that it was a shame to throw out that nice ribbon, the one that you had just gotten a hold of, now that you could use it. This is completely correct.

However, if you had not just thrown it out, you would not have remembered even having it. It would still be in its drawer or box and you would have chosen a different solution. That is what you will do now. You will find another solution now that might be even better.

Do it this way

Remember, it is about what you can do without, not what you can use.

"Ask, Can I live without…?"

We store many odds and ends because we say to ourselves, "They might come in handy one day." They are often small, worthless things such as the piece of cardboard from the back of a writing pad, the nice ribbon once used on a package, good advertising pens, key rings, cardboard boxes of various sizes, gift wrap, or the back of envelopes used as sticky notes. Feel free to add to the list.

Believe me, you will find another solution in the event that you actually do end up missing something after you have thrown it out. I guarantee that you will not be ruined. Once you start getting rid of the things that are irrelevant to your life, you will feel almost euphoric.

I have witnessed it many times and would love to be a fly on your wall, experiencing your joy and exhilaration.

Postcards

Many people still send greetings back home when they are on vacation. Why? Maybe it is a bit like Christmas cards. We have the opportunity to show that we are still alive. Or, is it for the sake of bragging? In the early days of tourism, this was probably the case. If nothing else, a great postcard can always make us daydream for a while.

Keep on sending cards, but there is no need for you to save them forever. While we are happy to be remembered, it does not mean that we have to hang on to them for eternity. The postcards represent the life and experience of the one sending it, not of you.

Do it this way

Once you have thanked the sender, the card has expired. Throw it away unless it is so nice that you want to frame it or use it as a bookmark. If you are not going to really use it, then throw it OUT. Do not put them on the refrigerator.

Gifts

Trust me, there are expiry dates on gifts and gratitude as well.

People give each other the weirdest things, things that no one wishes for, but everyone gives as friendly gestures. We keep them because we are afraid of offending the person who gifted it or because it might have been expensive. It can be anything from standard, boring gifts for the hostess to personal birthday presents.

If you do not care about the thing, if it does not make you happy, if the price or the person that gave it to you does not matter, it is not part of you.

Why should other people decide what we ought to own? I recognize that gifts are given with the best intentions. We all know how difficult it can be to come up with ideas for that perfect surprise. We do our best to make the recipient happy, no?

Honestly, most gifts are not fantastic ideas because we usually choose something simply because we need to come up with an idea, any idea. Even if a present really DOES show that the giver gave it a lot of thought, the purpose was to make you happy. If it does not make you happy, it is of no use to either of you.

You are not doing that person any favors if you keep something that will only make you feel bad or guilty because you are not quite as happy as they intended.

Remember in the future to only buy gifts that can be exchanged or enjoyed, such as chocolate, wine, flowers, or other perishable things.

Do it this way

If you get annoyed every time you look at something, the decision has already been made. You have to get rid of it before it drains you of more energy.

If you have nice, valuable things that others might appreciate, you can choose to give them away to happy and sincere recipients. But, be careful to avoid circulating more bad gifts.

If it is something that you do not even want to give away, there is only one thing to do: OUT.

Inherited things

Inherited things are usually way past their expiry date. Way, way past. The expiry date on an inherited item was no later than the day that the original owner died…

If you have ever inherited or emptied a residence, you know that there were only a few things that you would have fought to keep. This is how it should be. You have taken the rest of it because you either felt obligated or because it was 'too good to throw away'. Someone had to take it, so it was you.

Maybe you thought that your children would take some of it, but true to form, they did not! They politely declined the towels, bed linens, crocheted doilies, tablecloths, candlesticks, books, and porcelain vases.

Do it this way

I am guessing that your inheritance now lives in big boxes in the basement or attic and that you do not know how to get rid of it. But, getting rid of it is exactly what you need to do.

The rightful owners were happy with their things whilst they were able. All you have now is a guilty conscience because you do not love these items as the deceased did. But, you never wanted these things. They are not yours.

They do not make you happy and they are not part of your story. They simply have to get out of your life. NOW. There is no need to feel guilty anymore.

These are things that helped paint a picture of the person who owned them. You are not this person and the picture is not of you.

Dinnerware

There are an incredible number of old pieces of inherited dinnerware in our homes, at least in Danish homes. It is usually a large set of nice, once valuable dinnerware and accessories. They are used only for special occasions and are, therefore, quite significant. Very little has been broken. The porcelain producer, Royal Copenhagen, is doing a great job.

As you are deciding what to do with your own set, it comes down to how often you are really going to use it. Furthermore, with gold trim on many of the dishes, they are not dishwasher safe. Who would want the hassle of washing each by hand when the party is over?

Maybe Aunt Anna did, but she did not have a dishwasher and everything had to be washed by hand anyway. It did not make much difference what kind of dinnerware needed to be washed. It had to be done regardless. This is not the case today.

Think of how extensive a set of dinnerware for special guests was only 50 years ago. Just consider the number of salt and pepper shakers, sauce pots, potato dishes, sugar bowls, candlesticks, ashtrays, and many other quirky things typical for a collection.

We do not use many of these accessories today.

Do it this way

Be honest: Would you have purchased extra dinnerware sets for yourself if you had not been given these? It was not your choice to get the set when you did; it just landed on your shoulders.

Ask yourself if you even want to set the table with Aunt Anna's dinnerware. Sure, the individual plates and cups are beautiful, but as a huge set, is it an expression of you or how you would like to set the table for your guests today?

Remember, not all dinnerware is the same. If you were lucky enough to inherit a set of valuable pieces, check the market price before throwing it out or giving it away. If it is valuable, sell it, otherwise OUT or to the recycling.

It will not get any prettier or more valuable if you save it for a few years or ten. You can also be sure that it will not be used. If you were going to use it, it would have happened already.

Porcelain figurines and the other inherited things

Let us make it clear once again: Most of the things that you inherit you would not have wanted or chosen. The deceased might have appreciated these things, but it may have just been clutter. Things that you inherit can be put in the same category as gifts that you do not love.

The worst things to inherit are the ones that are directly entrusted to us by the widow or widower. What should you do when your aunt stubbornly insists that you take the incredibly horrific porcelain figure that was given to your deceased uncle by his company when he retired? Her intentions may have been good, but now you are stuck with it. You cannot hide it and you cannot destroy it as long as your aunt is still coming into your home.

She wanted to please you, but you never wanted this giant porcelain polar bear. Sure, it is elegant and probably also expensive, but it does not fit you or your home.

... Maybe your aunt was just trying to get rid of her own mess?

Do it this way

Make her happy and accept it.

But then, make yourself happy and get rid of it as soon as possible. You can only hope that her good manners keep her from asking about it. Only let things survive if you really want to use and then actually use them.

If it is fine kick-knacks that you want in your home, find different and varied ways to exhibit them. Use your beautiful crystal plates for dessert, the Christmas plates for holiday celebrations, and perhaps reframe the beautiful painting that you love so much.

The strategy is the same for everything that is inflicted upon us. If you love to look at them and know that they are valuable to you, you should definitely save them.

If not, well, you have probably guessed it already: OUT.

Memories

The little guy's first pacifier, travel brochures from a past trip, old concert tickets, and so on. Everything from the past belongs in the memories category, good things as well as bad ones.

Memories are attached to feelings and can make you shed a tear or ten. Some memories are so important that they should be saved, while others have less value. Believe it or not, memories also have expiry dates.

"The value of memories wears off over time"

Do not get me wrong; we must absolutely save the things that tell the positive story of our lives. It would certainly be sad if we were left with nothing attached to our memories.

We also have a certain responsibility to save things for future generations. Although Uncle Axel might not have left many good memories, he was still part of our history. We must preserve our history for the sake of our descendants. Maybe they will want to understand the family ties one day, which will not be possible if we've erased a few black sheep.

Even though we should remember to save our history, there is a limit to how much and what we should keep.

Do it this way

Focus on the three L's of cleanup: LIMIT, LIMIT, LIMIT.

We need to save only items that mark milestones in our lives. These are the things that stand as proof of experiences or events in our lives, like pictures that tell a story or things that trigger good feelings.

Nostalgia is a very important element of measurement, but use it positively. Nostalgia is closely associated with feelings of pain, looking back on experiences we are not able to relive, but will remain a part of history. Save the good memories and consider whether or not the bad ones may have reached their expiry dates.

You must limit yourself to things that really mean something positive to you or will serve as proof for your descendants.

Some things are more important than others. For example, the beautiful doll from Corsica that you bought when you were 12 years old may evoke precious memories that must be preserved. It might be worth using, or maybe it should be stored with other old memories to be displayed when the time is right. If not, then OUT.

That beer mug from the Harz was probably great once, but it might be time to press the limit button on that one and say goodbye. Make sure that you keep a close eye on how valuable these things are to you and only save the best.

Memories from our younger days

Memories from when we were young can easily take up a lot room on shelves and in the basement. I have seen lots of boxes in lots of basements, filled with notebooks, assignments, and books from back in business school.

Those kinds of things are memories that helped us become who we are today, and for that reason they are important to us.

Lots of vinyl records are also taking up a significant amount of room on shelves in basements and even in living rooms. These LPs might represent many experiences and feelings, but not even be playable anymore because the gramophone was thrown out years ago.

Do it this way

Go through all of your notes and pick out the ones that you know will not be missed. Stay strong and ask yourself how much proof you need of your hard work. If they are notes pertaining to professional knowledge, you will definitely be able to find new, updated versions online faster than finding the old ones in the basement.

Without a doubt, certain songs and LPs will evoke memories of both good and bad feelings. Go through your vinyl and if you need to save some of them, save only the very best memories.

You have probably saved many other things from when you were young. They are not all trophies that need to be passed on for the sake of posterity. Only keep the ones that are truly important to you, ones that you will enjoy seeing or hearing again.

It is not necessary to keep documentation for every minute of your life. Let go.

Collectables

Collectables are different from memories. Collectables are things that you collect just for the sake of collecting. The funniest, most amazing things can be collectables, from pens to alarm clocks, unique whiskey glasses to matchboxes, and much, much more. You are motivated by the sport of collecting. For some, the pursuit is the interesting part.

If you are missing an issue of a series, the process of finding that specific issue is exciting. Once in place, you will feel victorious because you have conquered the challenge and completed the series. The feeling that 'something is missing' is the driving force.

For others, the joy of collecting is about completing the whole. These kinds of hobbyists keep all of their books in order by numbers. I bet, however, that the joy is just temporary. Soon you will find a new collecting challenge that you must finish before you can have that fleeting feeling of completion again.

Do it this way

I assume that you are still reading along because you want to put an end to your clutter. If so, it will do you no good to hang on to the habit of collecting. Instead, look at what can be limited.

Ask yourself, how many of your collections were really just for fun and not because they are of actual value to you.

If you have valuable collections that you do not enjoy taking up room, consider whether or not they should be sold. Perhaps others are in pursuit of something that you have. If you collect beautiful whiskey glasses that make you happy, then show the world your true self by displaying them. Present them nicely and admit that this is your hobby. Remember, your home should reflect the richness of your personality.

Letting go of a collection could even benefit your relationship because the habit is often annoying to the other half. Think about it.

Expensive things

Things that were expensive, but no longer in use, stick to us. This is especially true for purchases that we regret and feel guilty about.

Maybe you had to own a piece of fitness equipment that did not get used like you promised yourself? Now it is scowling at you every time you pass by.

Maybe there was a fur coat that should have made you look really chic, but the lining felt wrong and animal welfare made it difficult to enjoy.

Or, you bought that microwave and then only used it for popcorn, which you no longer eat.

Feeling regretful for purchases happens even when you least expect it. Your intention was good, but the thing still does not fit into your everyday life. Now it is creating bad energy around you.

Do it this way

When things are not beneficial and enjoyable to you anymore, it is time to look at their expiry dates. These items are probably not becoming any more necessary or useful to you simply because you saved them. Your conscience will not find any relief from this either. If the thing is still intact and works properly, recycling could be a solution. Otherwise, get it OUT.

Ask yourself, how big a relief you would feel if it disappeared from your life? Make up your mind and enjoy the result. Admit that you regret the purchase and politely say thank you and goodbye. Your bad conscience is not doing you any good and you need to get rid of the thing causing it. Recycle it and let others benefit from the good that it could do. You have nothing more to give each other.

Exhausting things

Things that are large or bulky often stay longer than necessary.

It is difficult to get rid of pictures that are too large to even fit in the car to be taken away. This is even truer for furniture.

> *From my own world - At one point, I helped empty the house of a family member who had kept some very beautiful, but very heavy and outdated furniture from his grandparents. It was almost unbearable to let them go with that much history and beautiful craftsmanship. We rented a van and struggled with the heavy furniture. Of course, we had no room for them and they did not fit with our other furniture. It all ended up in the garage for a couple of years, until a charity organization picked it up...*

Do it this way

If the thing is valuable, let it be appraised by an expert who may even take it with the intention of selling it. You could ask your family, friends, and acquaintances if they would be interested in taking it. If anyone is interested, they can pick it up as soon as possible.

If all you can do is recycle an item, many second-hand businesses will pick things up free of charge. In my country, if it is valuable, you even get a tax receipt with a specified value to deduct from taxes as charity.

Ancient artifacts and furniture take a lot of our energy. The size alone is tiring. You could probably use the space for something else.

Broken things

Things break. That is how it is. It is the reason that the eternity machine has not been invented.

Some items we get repaired immediately, others require tools or skills that we do not possess.

When things are of a certain value, it increases our desire to repair them. However, when an item passes its expiry date, we tend to forget about it. We find a different solution. We buy a new version, which quickly turns out to have other advantages and we never return to the broken one.

The lawnmower might be left in the dark with only one metal pin missing in the wheel. Maybe the picture frame only needs a drop of glue, the drying rack only needs a new string, or the broom, with the head that keeps falling off, simply needs a new screw.

The list can be endless.

Do it this way

If it broke recently and there is still hope, repair it immediately. The two-week rule also applies to broken things.

If the damage happened long ago and it has been left broken, increasing your guilt every time you meet, there is only one solution. OUT! Face it; you two are over.

Are some of your children's toys in need of a loving hand? Decide first whether or not they are worth the trouble. There is a reason that you did not do it already.

Maybe the thing is so insignificant that the only benefit you will find in fixing it is the thrill of your own thriftiness or maybe the child and toy have grown apart already. Choose how you want to spend your time.

If the economic and entertainment value is in clear contrast with the value of your effort, consider whether the thing should simply disappear from the face of the earth. If, however, a little effort could be beneficial in the future, put the repair on your to-do list.

Abandoned or borrowed things

The wardrobe or the piano was too big for the new apartment that your friends moved into 10 years ago and so, it ended up at your place.

Whatever the children left when they moved away from home is also there: furniture, toys, school notes, skis, boots, festival equipment, and so on.

Though you may have enough room, there is no reason for you to store other people's things for years. They have to take responsibility for their own clutter. It is their energy taking up room in your mind.

Your children also have to learn these cleanup principles, which you have so admirably started now. Everybody must take care of his or her own stuff.

Do it this way

You should demand that large things be picked up quickly by using a two-week rule. You can make a threatening remark that you will throw out whatever it is or sell it for your own profit in return for storing it all this time. Some things might just be worthless and can be thrown out with peace of mind. Do it.

If the children have left things that they are not going to use again, you all have to agree on what to do with them. If it is temporary storage because their place is small, that is an entirely different matter.

If there are things you have borrowed from other people, of course, the owner should be involved. Does he want it back? Can it be given away or thrown out? If borrowed items have become a positive part of your home, make a deal with the owner to buy them at an affordable price. This way you can have peace of mind, knowing that it is legally yours.

Books

Danish Hygge pairs well with books. Sitting on the couch, wrapped in a plaid, with hot chocolate in a cup, disappearing into a book, it all evokes the Hygge mood.

In Denmark, the book-tsunami started 35-40 years ago and the wave is ongoing. It was around this time that bookcases became acceptable. Book clubs had a field day, with their book packages washing over us. We collected books in ever-increasing numbers and appeared more and more well-read. Some books were really good, but not all. The problem was that they actually looked quite nice in the bookcase, with their beautiful spines and the gold font under the dust jacket.

The interest in books is here to stay, fortunately. However, it does not make our collections smaller or better.

Do it this way

Books are physical things, but we do not have to keep them forever. After we have read them, we have taken all of the pleasure that we can. There is nothing left in the book for us. It has expired.

We are talking about the fact that all books take up space. Am I completely wrong in assuming there are also a couple of boxes in the basement or attic? Perhaps books that you inherited…

Maybe there are books that you never properly finished. You made it to page 67, but it had nothing more to give. Believe me, it will not be more interesting after spending several years in your bookcase.

Keep the good books that you would like to own forever and will read again. Of course, books that are beautiful or otherwise show your personality should stay.

Ask yourself, which books you can definitely do without? Go through your bookcase several times. Once you think that you are done cutting down the amount, do it one more time, while asking yourself:

"What would happen, if I never saw this book again?"

Even second-hand shops do not want some of these cast-offs. Let them be passed on, either to other bookworms or for combustion.

Pictures and frames

There is no escaping the fact that our homes clearly show who we are. The pictures that we choose to hang on the walls show what kind of people we are. They tell something about our cultural background, our education, and our interests, even if the picture is abstract.

Pictures are part of our perspective of the world. We look at them every day, whether we are aware of it or not. When we choose to hang a picture on the wall, it is because it gives us something, in one way or another. We would never dream of hanging up something ugly. Pictures give us energy.

"There is an expiry date on pictures as well"

The day we take a picture down from the wall indicates the end of its life with us. Its usefulness is finished. We have moved beyond it. However, because we have held on to it for many years, maybe through many phases of our lives, we do not have the heart to get rid of it.

Keeping in mind future possibilities, we have chosen to put the picture away. It could be of use again one day. I have seen many doors, in many homes that were unable to fully open because of pictures stored in various places.

Do it this way

I invite you to take a thorough look at your pictures and ask yourself the following question for each one:

"How will this picture contribute to my future?"

It would certainly be a great relief to simply take a deep breath and get rid of it. Consider whether or not it is still nice enough to simply be hung elsewhere. Many bathrooms, for example, could do with a little cheering up.

The pictures that survive must really be valuable to you. Make sure that they are properly stored, including protection at the corners. If you do not take good care of them, you might as well get rid of them immediately.

Once you have cleaned up properly, you would not dream of hanging a damaged picture on your wall. It would create clutter. When you clean up, you boost your energy. Things that are not maintained will reflect a different '*you*'; a '*you*' that departed when you chose a life of order and caring for yourself and your belongings. You will get more out of life when you have more order and clarity. Look forward to this.

Photos

Although prints are a dying species, there are still millions of pictures lying around our homes. The vast majority of them are put directly into albums. These pictures were being taken, printed immediately, admired, and then forgotten.

The joy and anticipation of reliving the event is over and the pile of pictures is now just a source of guilt instead. What exactly do you do with all of the pictures aside from neatly putting them in an album?

Do it this way

You should hold off with the photo album for a bit. Instead, buy two archive boxes with lids. The size should fit your pictures. They are often readily available and you can find them at supermarkets or other stores near you.

Grab the first and best photo pocket. Go through all of the pictures. Throw out any that are blurry, distorted, without any real motif, or show repetitive subjects from a slightly different angle or just a few seconds later.

If you are in the habit of traveling to the same place over and over, you will also find yourself shooting the same motifs. We all have our favorite spots.

When you have cut down the collection to the absolute minimum, label the back of each photo with the year, a short note about the occasion, and maybe who or what is in the picture.

The subjects of your pictures, particularly if they are people, are quite important from a historical perspective. You might be fully aware that it is your cousin Karen sitting there to the far right. However, when your children or grandchildren find the box in 50 years, they will be happy to know that the one in the fancy summer dress was cousin Karen from mom's side of the family.

Genealogy is here to stay. We want to know our roots and origin. Do your descendants that favor.

Now, fold a piece of paper and place it in the file box. Write the year at the top and possibly the occasions, if it will help in identifying the box. E.g.:

2008
- Skiing holidays in Austria
- Michael's 40th birthday
- Christmas
- Misc.

You will be surprised how many pictures a box can store.

Photo album – here it comes

Forget all about putting the pictures into photo albums for now. You have gone this long without fulfilling your dream to put them away, so why now, when you are busy cleaning up...?

The box is your tool. By using archive boxes as storage for photos, you can get in control of them in a short time. However, if you realize later that you would prefer to store your photos in an album, you now have them in order and can put them together quickly. If the day should come when you suddenly have the time and desire, you are ready. Otherwise, let it be.

The negatives

Once, many years ago copies were made for everyone in the pictures. After a 50th birthday, photos were sent to every guest. This is not done anymore. If shared at all, it would be online.

This means that you do not actually need the negatives anymore. You have probably already made the necessary copies, so you can throw out the negatives.

What are the odds that your house will burn down and you will need to make new copies? If a fire occurs, what are the chances that your pictures will be destroyed but not your negatives, especially if they are stored in the same photo pocket…?

If you decide to save them, store them separately. Before you go knocking on a neighbor's door, keep in mind that we cannot simply move our clutter into other people's homes.

I am guessing that you have your negatives with the pictures and have never used them. So, get them OUT.

CDs

Nowadays, many people download music and the rest of the world will surely learn eventually. For those who are still behind the times, CDs tend to live in strange-looking bookcases and racks and the equally strange collections tend to grow every year.

We all have our favorites, albums that make us happy when we play them over and over again, year after year. Please keep them, even though other people might not love them quite as much, that is their problem.

We are going to look at the rest now.

Do it this way

Not all CDs are worth saving. Sorry.

Start by going through the collection and getting rid of the ones that are not worth hearing again. Remember to toss the scratched ones that make the music skip. Forget the guilt and the things that you regret buying.

At IKEA, for example, you can buy excellent cardboard boxes with specific dimensions, suitable for CDs. Go out and buy some.

Next, buy some thin, soft CD pockets in plastic or paper. They are available in black and white and can be found many places, including well-stocked supermarkets. Remove each CD and booklet from the hard, plastic cover. Put them into the thin pockets and place them in the boxes, alphabetically or by genre.

If necessary, fill a box with only your favorite music.

Consider whether now is the time to put all of the music on your computer or use the options for online streaming. By doing so, you can still use your good speakers. There are many possibilities. Ask an expert.

DVDs

DVDs are getting cheaper and cheaper and are published faster and faster, while our collections just grow and grow.

It is worth remembering that DVDs are slightly different than CDs. We are able to listen to music over and over again, but with movies there are only a few that we watch more than once.

When we pay to go see a film, we pay for the experience and this expires as we walk out of the cinema. If we buy a DVD, we do not get rid of it after we watch it. We save it, often regardless of the quality.

Promise me that you will only save your very favorite DVDs, ones that you will want to watch forever.

Do it this way

Ask yourself if you really expect to watch this DVD again. If so, it should be within a year. It is not that you absolutely have to do a movie weekend marathon before the year is over, but it will give you a sense of where this DVD is placed in your priorities.

"Life is too short for bad movies"

Save your favorites and other classics by storing them in the same kind of pockets and boxes as the CDs. Get rid of the rest. Keep in mind the possibility that you could donate them.

Electronics, mobile phones, cables etc.

When you buy new electronics they come with lots of extra things such as cables, adapters, chargers and so on. Often, once you buy your new toy, you move it directly into a large, pre-existing pile and soon, everything is entangled and it is impossible to sort out.

"Old electronics and their cables are true agony"

I have seen many boxes filled to the point of bursting with equipment and accessories because nobody knew where they belonged.

Do it this way

Technology changes quickly and before we know it, we need new devices. That is reality. But, there was nothing wrong with the old computer or flat screen TV when you bought the new one. Why on earth should it be thrown out? You never know if you may need it someday, somewhere in your home.

Old electronics that end up thrown in the basement or in the guestroom have to be thrown OUT. Once we have become accustomed to new technology, it feels almost unnatural to go back to an old model. That is not how we do it.

Electronics, of one kind or another, hit their expiry dates with a proper bang. As soon as the new equipment is being unpacked and installed, your time with the old model has ended. Forget about giving it to the children and grandchildren, they are even more demanding! Give it to charity instead.

An extra piece of good advice

When buying new equipment, keep the manual and spare parts in a small plastic bag and label it with the date and model.

Should you need any of the pieces, it will be easy to find. If you do not need it anymore, it is much easier to clean up if you know what is in the bag.

Unfinished hobby projects

Ugh! This is one of the worst blocks because we are dealing with our own shattered expectations. We thought we could do it, but the project was left uncompleted.

Unfinished handiwork and hobbies take up a lot of room: the uncompleted jacket, the jersey with knitting needles still in it, and all of the painting supplies you bought when you planned to become a skilled hobby painter.

For some reason, we think that we have much more time in the winter to finish these projects. It just does not happen. The number of hours is still the same in the wintertime. In addition, we are busy during the winter, taking French lessons, doing yoga and Pilates, a million different things take up our time.

Honestly, we are busy with many of our hobby projects only for the sake of the project and not to see the result. It is in our nature and it should be allowed. Everything has a purpose.

If you choose to go for a walk, it is because you want some fresh air and exercise. If you read a book, it is for recreational purposes. Knitting is for the pleasure, the challenge, and for de-stressing.

However, if we spend a lot of money buying yarn for a sweater that we hope to enjoy working on for many hours, we end up feeling guilty when it was never completely finished. The yarn was not exactly cheap. It is also a shame that it is left unfinished because it did not turn out as we had planned.

Do not feel self-conscious because, if you find knitting enjoyable, it is pure therapy and worth every penny. However, the day that you stop working on it and leave it untouched, when the guilt starts to come out, then it is past the expiry date. You have had your fun together and time for Danish Hygge with this particular knitting project has ended.

Oddly enough, we do not feel guilty about the expenses associated with many other hobbies. When you spend money on TV licensing and various TV packages, playing golf, no one demands results and proof of proper usage of the subscription.

Do it this way

On a scale from 1-10, ask yourself how likely it is that you will ever finish your knitting.

The answer must be at least an 8 for your completion to be just a tad likely. If the answer is a 7 or lower, you should get rid of it.

"Say thanks for being good company, close your eyes, and throw it all out"

Do not unravel the knitting with the intention of using the yarn again. Every time you see it, you will feel bad and it will deny you the pleasure of buying new yarn for a new project. You will always be held back by that last, uncompleted project. It will never feel like a new project and we need new projects. Men fix. Women create.

You will experience great relief by throwing out all of the unfinished projects that have only been a source of guilt, perhaps for many years.

If your answer was above an 8 on the scale, then add the project to your checklist and finish it within two weeks. If it takes any longer, you will forget about it again.

"Help! My Husband is a Collector"

Women are the majority of the audience at my lectures. If a man has snuck in, there are two possibilities: either, his wife has more or less forced him because she thought he could learn something, or he has joined voluntarily and is committed 100%.

When a man has agreed to attend for the sake of peace on the home front, he does not present much to work with. His arms are crossed and he will rationalize his behavior.

In contrast, the men who join voluntarily are highly motivated to start clearing out their clutter. I have received the loveliest letters and emails from men who have participated in the lectures, explaining how a new world has opened up to them. Nothing could make me happier.

For men, identity is very important and it is linked to the things that surround them: cars, stereos, lawn mowers, gas or coal barbeques in several varieties, magazines, collectable items, and much more.

When the husbands have gone outside during the break, women have asked me many times, "What should I do? My husband will not clean up and he collects everything."

This is a tough one, but planning it out carefully can solve the problem.

Do it this way

I will not argue one method over the other in advance, but I will introduce you to a few different ways to put an end to a man's clutter. I am sorry that I am using the term 'man' for this, but the male sex is, in the majority, very stubborn when talking about clutter. Sorry. Should you find yourself in the opposite situation, with a stubborn wife, you probably get the message anyway.

Method 1

Start by cleaning up, not his things, but your own. Keep going and ask him for help getting rid of the heavy, large items.

Thank him nicely for helping you and then say, *"I feel so wonderful now that this and that are gone."* I would be surprised if he did not gradually start cleaning up his own mess. Keep in mind - a man should perceive this as his own good idea. It will probably be a slower process than you would wish for, but keep calm.

Method 2

Have a good, reasonable talk, where you are both strictly forbidden to argue. Plan for a suitable time. It will not work if he just sat down to watch the final match of his favorite sport or is tired from a long day at work.

Men's listening abilities deteriorate significantly when they are stressed or occupied with something else. Stay calm.

Try Sunday at dinner or any other time that is likely to be a bit quieter.

Say, *"Michael, I would like to talk to you about something. It is something that means a lot to me and I need to let you in on it."*

At this point, he will be a bit nervous and uncomfortable. He needs to know that he can safely continue listening.

Say, *"I do not want to divorce you or have you polish the silver.* (small pause) *However, I need a little more order around me. I need to talk about how we can find a solution together."*

If your husband is like most men, he will immediately say, *"Well, dearest Louise, you could just start cleaning up. It is your mess....!"*

Dear fellow sister, in this moment you must keep your temper and speak calmly. Stick to the matter and continue.

Say, *"I know that I am not the best at keeping things orderly, but would it be OK with you if I start and you help me once in a while?"*

He cannot say no to this. Gently continue.

Say, *"I have found that I feel better about myself when I have a clear understanding of what we have in our home. You have many things that you collect and I have many things that I am also happy with, but it would be really nice if you would help me get a better idea of where things are."*

Breathe and continue, *"Can we make a deal to each keep our things separately, with your stuff here and my stuff there? Would that be OK with you?"*

He will answer, *"Yes, just do not throw any of mine out. Was that all?"*

Mission accomplished, almost. Progress has at least been made.

Say, *"Yes and thank you for helping out. It means a lot to me. When do you think we should start?"*

It is important that, in his mind, the problem lies with you and the solution with him. I know that it is a little manipulative, but it works here and in other situations as well.

Method 3

Move his stuff to the garage or basement. You can at least close the door after that. Then, call a shrink.

The Permanent Order

So far so good, but do not think that everything is done just because you have sorted through your belongings. To clear clutter and to maintain order is two different things. Now you must employ new habits in your life, or else all of that trouble will go to waste. That would be a shame.

"Clutter is like a weed. You have to keep it down or it will take control."

Clearly, there are some routines in your daily life that you will have to change. The good news is that it does not hurt and is not as difficult as you might think. Your task is just to think a little differently.

It is easier than you think

Many clutter-heads think that orderly people run around all day, cleaning up. They could not be more wrong. Orderly people have simply realized that clutter steals too much energy. It must, therefore, be kept to a minimum.

"We all have clutter. The trick is to do something about it here and now!"

The secret behind everyday order

Speaking of daily disorder, I expect that you have gotten every expired thing in your home under control. I do not mean that I expect you to have thoroughly cleaned out your home, but that you have superficially organized everything that has ended up in the wrong place during the day or week.

The secret is to keep active clutter from becoming passive clutter. Once you have finished something, it must be cleaned up, even on a small scale.

Imagine that every task that you perform runs in circles. You start one place and end in the same location. Each time you finish one round everything should be back in place, ready for another round. Some circles overlap, but they still have their own course. All circles are chores, tasks, or projects in a closed cycle. They always have a start and an end. Once the chore is finished, it has reached its expiration.

"Make sure to always leave an orderly trail"

This way, you can greatly reduce the amount of time that you spend cleaning up after yourself. You can better invest your time because you will not return to the clutter twice or ten times before finishing the cleanup. You just need to continuously keep your trail in order once you finish a chore or task.

If you do not clean up afterwards, the task will hang in the air until it is finished.

Close the circles behind you

Uncompleted things are like open programs on a computer, they take up space and energy, whether you are using them or not. By closing the task immediately, you can use your time and energy on something else.

The circles of a day could look like this:

Good morning

The night is over. The circle is completed once you shake the pillow and duvet and put it neatly on the bed. Handle the bedroom with care so that it will be nice to return to in the evening. This is the day's first well-done task.

The bathroom

A visit to the bathroom requires lots of equipment. Once you have finished in the bathroom for the morning, end the task by putting everything that you used back in place. Close the circle. Make sure, in advance, that the storage and structure are in order. It should be easy to clean up after yourself each day.

Children

Your next project is waking up the children. Let them experience how closing circles is a natural part of the morning ritual.

Breakfast

It is always easy to take out everything that you need for a task. The trick is getting everything back in place. Do not leave anything on the kitchen table after breakfast. Clean up COMPLETELY. Put away the oatmeal and the used cups and glasses. Do not leave them in the sink. Clear it all.

It does not get better or easier if you leave it out. As a matter of fact, you will enjoy coming home to a neat kitchen.

Send your family out for the day; drop off the kids and say goodbye to your husband. In the morning the family spreads out towards all four corners of the world. Once I asked my mother why she waved goodbye to my father and she answered, "What if I never saw him again..." Oops, I had not thought of that at the age of 10. Make sure to close the goodbye circle as well, no matter where we say goodbye to each other.

The entranceway

Home again. Outerwear must be hung up; shoes and boots must be in place. This is the circle when coming home. Make sure to have plenty of storage solutions so that everyone in the family knows where their things belong.

Remember to use seasonal boxes to store the outerwear that is not currently in use. If there is not enough space in your home, rent a few square meters in the city.

Shopping

Bags with groceries must be emptied and put away. Remember to fold the bags neatly. A crumpled bag is not nice to look at and certainly not a picture of you and your new, tidy world. A nicely folded bag in a basket or drawer is much more inviting. Close the circle.

Cooking

A meal is a big circle that consists of many smaller circles. Constantly focus on the individual task before you. When the potatoes are peeled, finish the circle by getting rid of the bag, washing the potato peeler, and returning it to the drawer. Once the other vegetables are sorted, finish those circles too. Put the remaining groceries in place, wash the utensils, and put them away before you start the next circle.

"Constantly end the circle before starting the next"

When the food is done, end the cooking circle by clearing out everything that you have used. Also, wash the pots and equipment before sitting down at the table. Complete the circle before you start the next one – cozy dinnertime. Remember, the children are a major resource when helping out, even if they think otherwise.

A cozy evening

The children are in bed. TV. Tea. Goodies. In any order. Again, look at it all as circles, to be completed.

Goodnight

When you reach bedtime, make sure that the big circle of today closes: clean up in the living room, fold the blanket, and put the teacups in the dishwasher. Get ready to open the circle with a good feeling the next day. Enjoy getting into bed where the previous night's circle was closed with care and is now welcoming you.

I know that there are many more chores in all of our lives. However, I believe that I have listed enough examples for you to understand my intention. Once the task is finished, it has reached its expiration; it must be closed and come to an end, no matter what you are doing, when you are doing it, or why.

The "good" excuses

I know that you may be in a hurry one morning and think, "Never mind the cleanup." In the evening, you could be dead tired and give up cleaning before you go to bed.

Of course, you might feel that caring for yourself means going to bed now instead of cleaning the living room after spending time there during the evening. But then, you are simply pushing the clutter into the next day. You will have to wake up to a messy couch and coffee rings on the living room table. It is highly unlikely that you want to start the next day with work left over from yesterday. You need to start a lot of new things today. Suddenly, you have set a precedent of putting off the cleaning up in front of you until you have the time and desire to do something about it. The negative circle has started. Avoid it.

Remember, you are caring for yourself when you make sure that the living room is inviting and ready to start a new day with you. You will love being able to start the day saying, "Wow, it is so nice in here," simply because you pulled yourself together and spent five minutes the night before cleaning up.

This is such a small investment for such a great feeling.

You can be dead certain that procrastinating will never increase your desire to clean. On the contrary, there is nothing like unclosed circles to take up your energy and time.

> *From my own world - I once had an English teacher whose name was Miss Widding. She was a little, old, cigar-smoking lady who drove a Volkswagen. When an English assignment had not been carried out to the fullest, or for that matter was missing, she yelled:*
>
> *"Whatever you do, do it fully, never in bits and pieces!"*
>
> *Now I know what she meant...*

The Secret to Order

The secret to order consists of:

- *Perspective and Surplus*
- *Management and Care*
- *Storage and Structure*
- *Order and Cleanup*

Perspective and Surplus

In order for you to maintain your level of organization and get the awesome feeling of having surplus time and energy, you need perspective.

Perspective – Good perspective will give you control. You will know exactly where everything lives and stays and you will always be able to put them away. If the picture of your home is disturbed by disorder, you do not have the correct perspective. The less clutter, the better your view will be. Nothing can hide from your eagle eye.

Surplus of time and energy – Once you have a clear view, you will also experience a surplus of time and energy in your life. In good conscience, you can take time off, invite guests over, or read a book. You decide. You do not have to feel guilty for not cleaning up. It is over now.

Management and Care

Management and care are related. You cannot manage to care for yourself if you do not have the energy to even try. To manage is to care. To care is to manage.

Management - The more energy you have, the easier any task will be. Do it immediately, before the task grows. No one else will do it for you, so you might as well do it for yourself right now. The time will never be better. Manage it!!! Manage cleaning up immediately.

Care - When you care for your things, you also care for yourself. Open your eyes and see what you have surrounded yourself with. Really look. Determine right away what should happen to each individual thing. Follow each into place. Do it now. Care. Imagine if they could talk and thank you!

Storage and Structure

Storage and structure are the same and yet not. Storage is just a place to be but, structure is about storing your things conveniently.

Storage - All things have to stay somewhere. Talk with your things and ask them where they live. If you do not have proper storage, they quickly become clutter. It is necessary to have enough shelves, cupboards and drawers, but not too many.

Structure - Structure means that your things are conveniently placed according to their function or the needs that they fulfill. If you cook in the kitchen, but your recipes live in the office, what good are they doing? Extra toilet paper should be by the toilet, not stored away in the basement.

Order and Cleanup

Order and cleanup are also naturally dependent on each other. If you do not clean up, well then, you do not have order. On the other hand, if you have order, it is much easier to clean up.

Order - Order does not happen by itself. It requires focus and attention. The secret is to maintain order at all times. It is easier than you think, as long as you are observant of your things all of the time. Every day. Keep focused and finish everything that you do completely. Close the circles immediately.

Cleanup – Cleaning up is a necessary part of life. Just like brushing your teeth, cooking, laundry, or a thousand other things. You must see pleasing yourself as a positive, necessary thing. If you do not clean up, slowly but surely, you will lose energy. Cleaning up is added to your life's account of time and energy; you gain time and energy by maintaining order and cleaning up.

The Secret to Danish Hygge

You cannot buy Danish Hygge. No one can box it up for you, and you cannot find it in a store. It is a way of life and has to grow within and around you.

Some of the main ideas are:

Moments filled with awareness, care, focus, peace, coziness, passion, trust, loyalty, eye contact, listening, and relaxation. But, there is much more.

It involves things like: aesthetic surroundings spiced with candlelight, warm materials, fur, wood, and warmth. But, even that is not everything.

Enjoying a cup of your favorite tea or hot chocolate or having homemade dinner with good friends eaten at a table set with care. These are some part of it; they will point you in the right direction.

Hygge is perfect moments of Joy, Peace and Harmony.

A few things to start with:

- *First of all, you have to declutter to create space for Danish Hygge.*
- *Always light candles when it is a bit dark.*
- *Always be comfortably warm.*
- *Remember care and awareness, because it is so important.*
- *Be the perfect Hygge friend filled with peace, acknowledgement and attention.*
- *Dine with friends for hours at home.*
- *Decorate the dining table with candles and flowers.*

Sign up to my newsletter to hear about my upcoming book: The Secret to Danish Hygge: How to create, live and enjoy the Danish lifestyle: lenabentsen.com

The Ten Commandments

In this book, we have gone through a lot of good advice about how to purge unnecessary things. You must, of course, continue to focus on this. Let us summarize so that you will remember everything:

- *You must ask each item, "where do you live?", and respond accordingly.*
- *You must know that everything has an expiry date.*
- *You must finish your tasks and close the circles.*
- *You must always focus on one thing at a time.*
- *You are not allowed to export your clutter.*
- *You must let go and live happily without.*
- *You must know the value of purpose or pleasure.*
- *You must never postpone cleaning up.*
- *You must remember that cleaning up is a part of life.*
- *You must remember that every step is towards freedom.*

May the freedom and feeling of Danish Hygge be with you.

Afterword

Dear reader, this is all I want to teach you for now. I hope that you will enjoy and use every bit of information I have offered, and that it will bring you the order you are seeking. Congratulations, YOU are the one achieving the reward: FREEDOM.

Sign up to my newsletter, and we will stay in touch: lenabentsen.com

If you have enjoyed the book, I will be so pleased if you would review it on Amazon.

If you have comments, please feel free to contact me here: contact@lenabentsen.com

Other Books by Lena Bentsen

<u>Coming soon in English:</u>

- *The Secret to Danish Hygge: How to create, live and enjoy the Danish lifestyle*

- *Enjoy Your Kitchen: How to revamp, optimize and organize in 5 easy steps*

- *Enjoy Your Wardrobe: How to declutter and discover your treasures*

- *Enjoy Your Work Desk: How to regain control by decluttering and organizing*

- *Kill the Hamster Wheel: 5 magic circles for an enhanced everyday life*

- *Flirt for Love and Life: 11 ways to boost your self-worth and become the best YOU*

- *Christmas Without Stress: How to survive December with Danish Hygge*

Learn more: www.lenabentsen.com

21105505R00078

Printed in Poland
by Amazon Fulfillment
Poland Sp. z o.o., Wrocław